DOG-GONE-IT

DOG-GONE-IT

WILLOW CREEK PRESS®

Published by Willow Creek Press, Inc.
P.O. Box 147, Minocqua, Wisconsin 54548

Printed in China

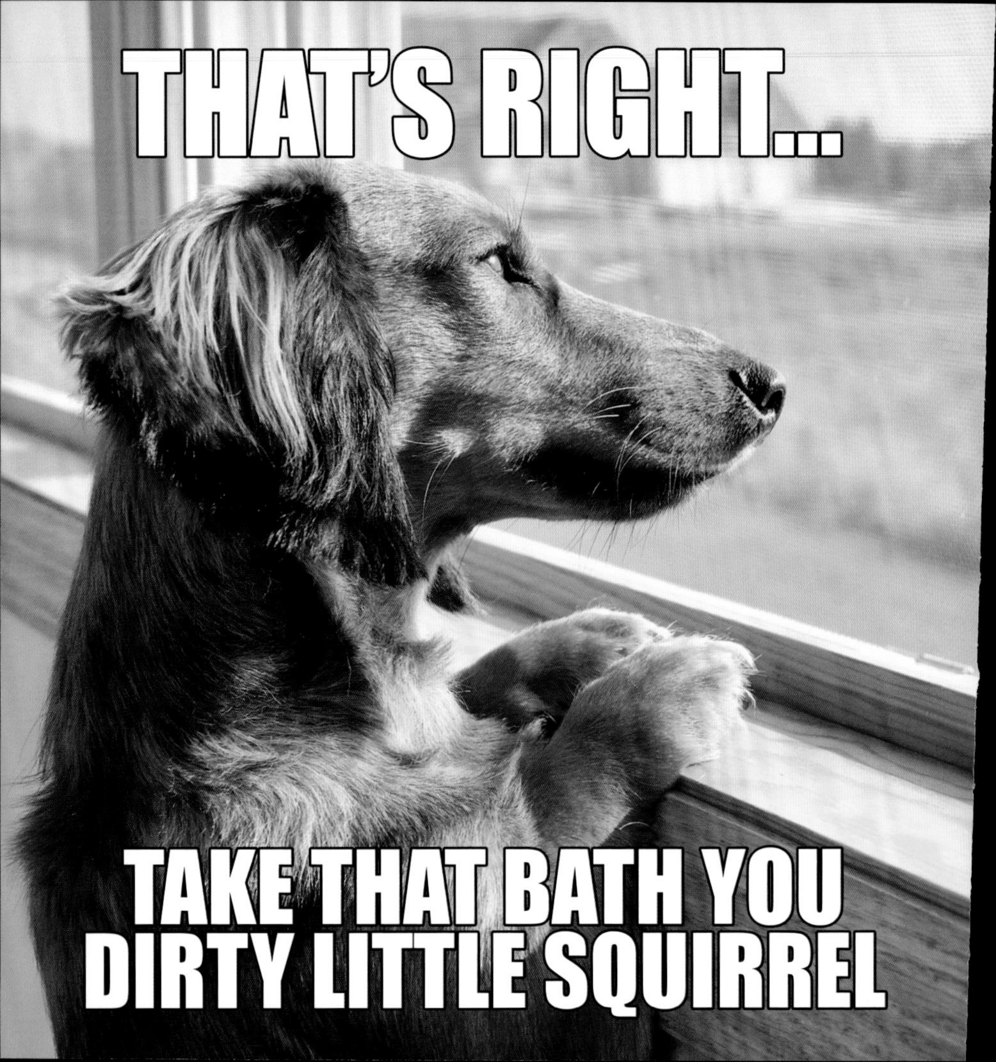
THAT'S RIGHT...
TAKE THAT BATH YOU
DIRTY LITTLE SQUIRREL

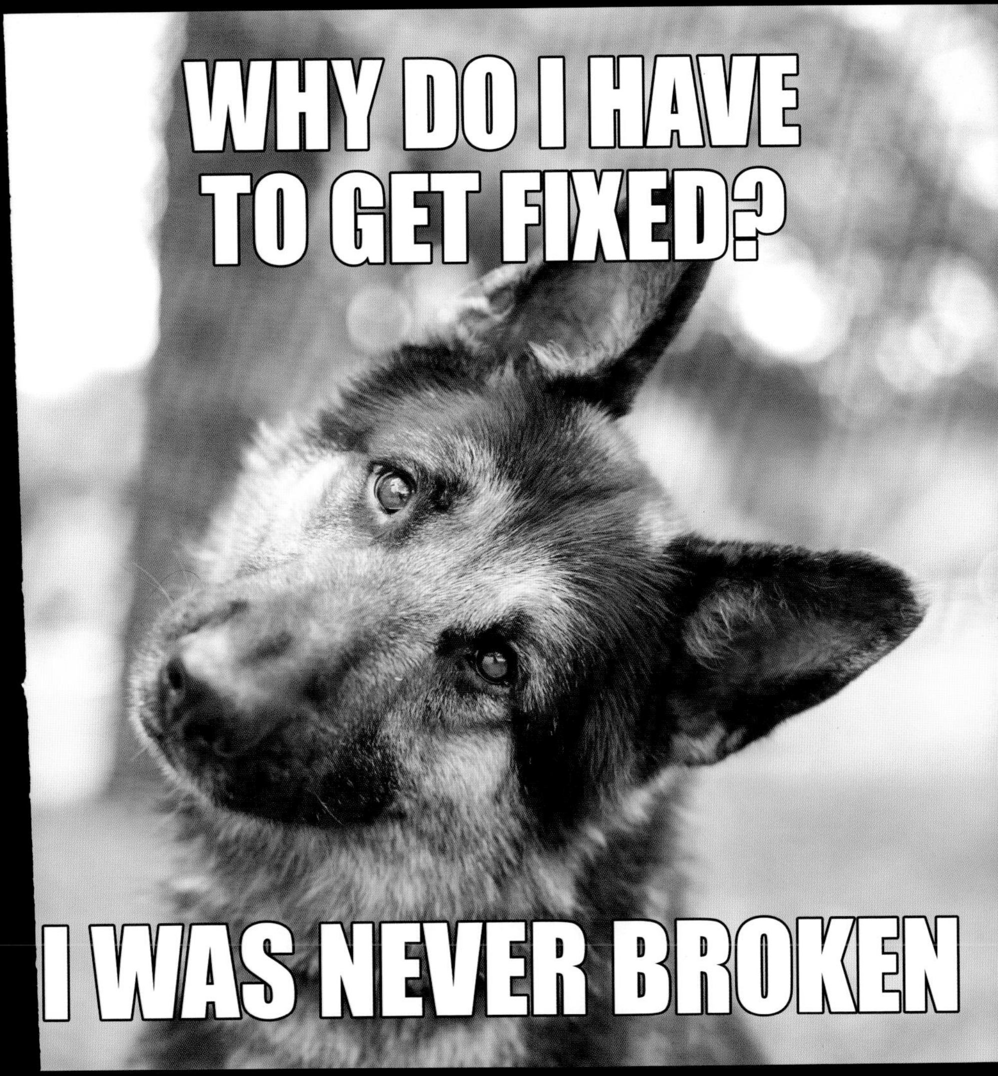
WHY DO I HAVE
TO GET FIXED?
I WAS NEVER BROKEN

CAN YOU TAKE ME ON A WALK

PLEASE!!!!!

EXCUSE ME,

BUT ARE YOU GOING
TO EAT THAT?

SAW YOU PETTING THE NEIGHBORS DOG...
DO YOU WANT TO TELL ME WHAT THAT WAS ABOUT?

YOU DO WHAT

IN THERE?!

I JUST CHEWED ALL YOUR SHOES

SO YOU NEVER HAVE TO LEAVE ME AGAIN

I'M FROM TECH SUPPORT

I'M HERE TO DELETE YOUR COOKIES

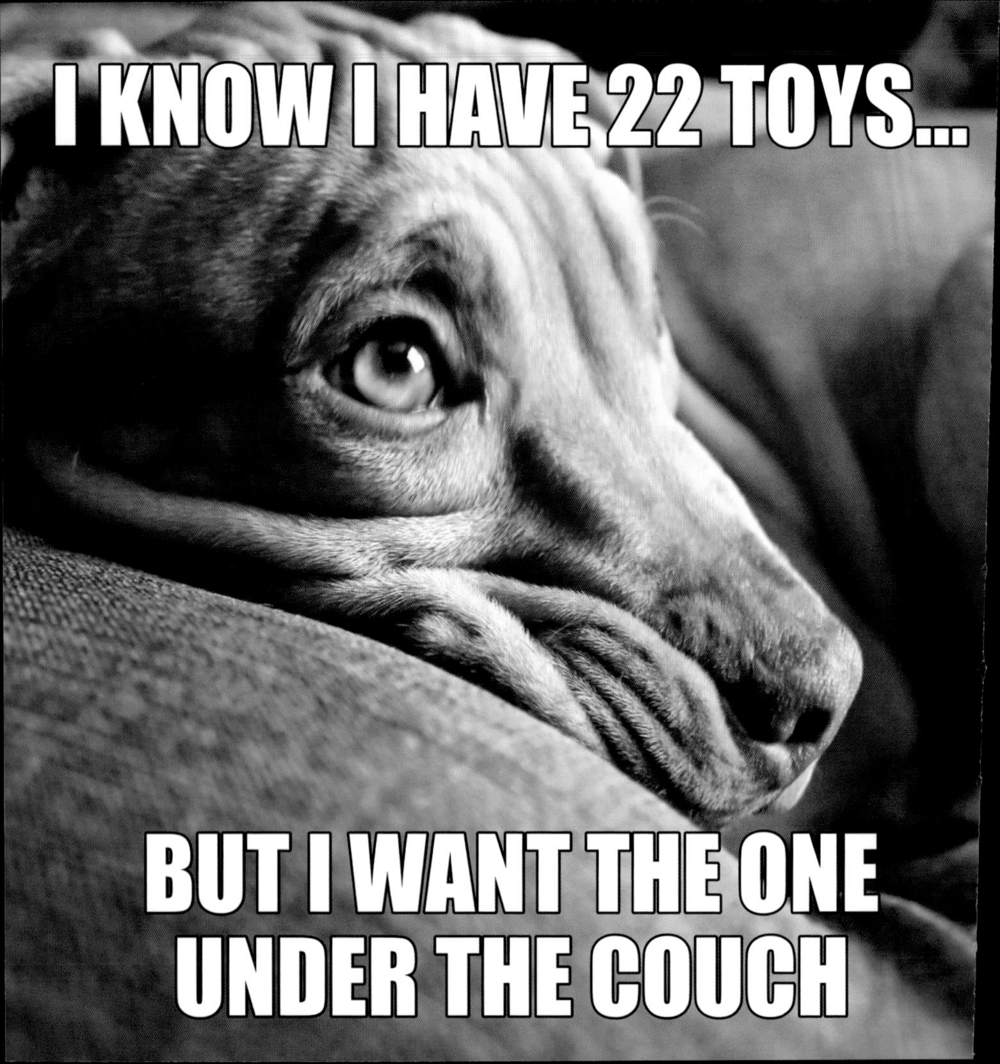
I KNOW I HAVE 22 TOYS...
BUT I WANT THE ONE
UNDER THE COUCH

I'M SORRY PAL, I HEARD YOUR FAMILY GOT A CAT

TODAY IS THE DAY

I'M GOING TO GET THAT TAIL

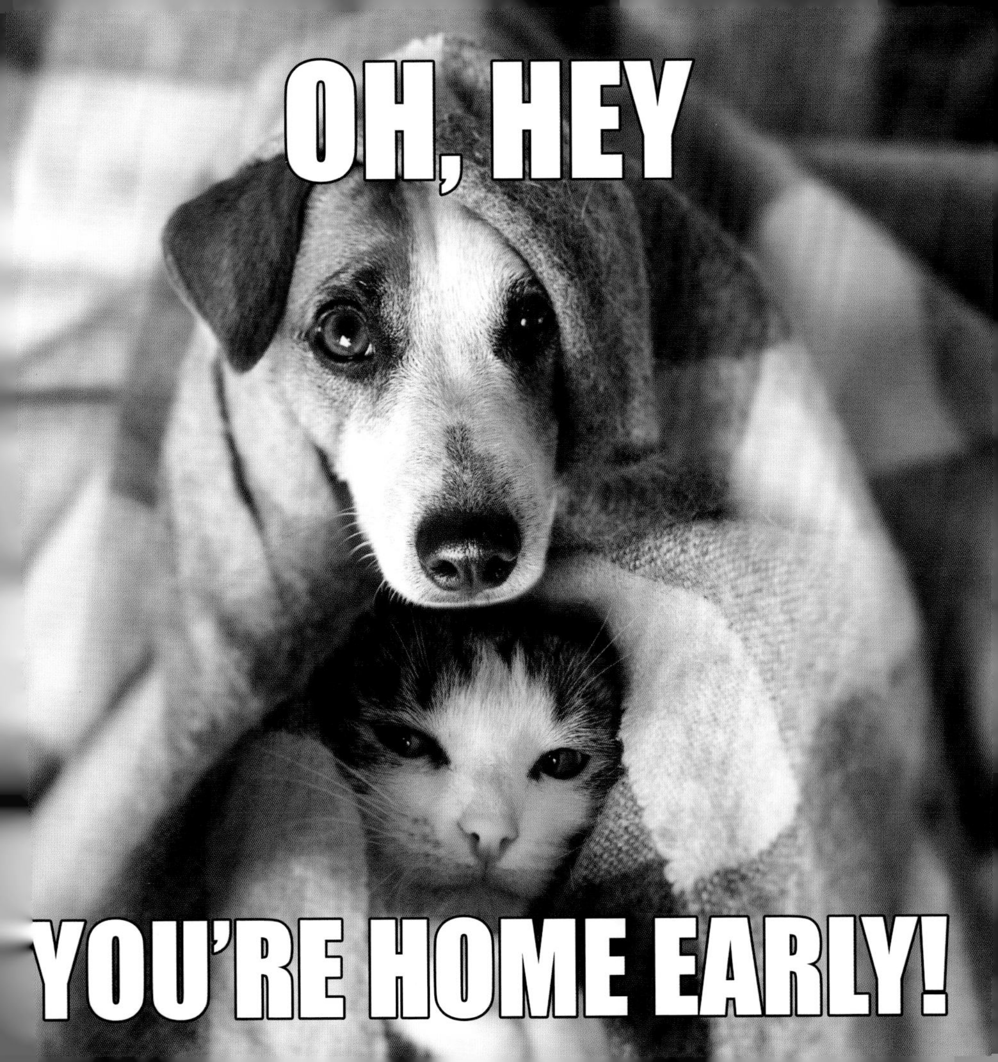
OH, HEY
YOU'RE HOME EARLY!

ESCAPE ATTEMPT

10% COMPLETE

LONG STORY SHORT
YOU'RE OUT OF TOILET PAPER

BONE APPETIT!

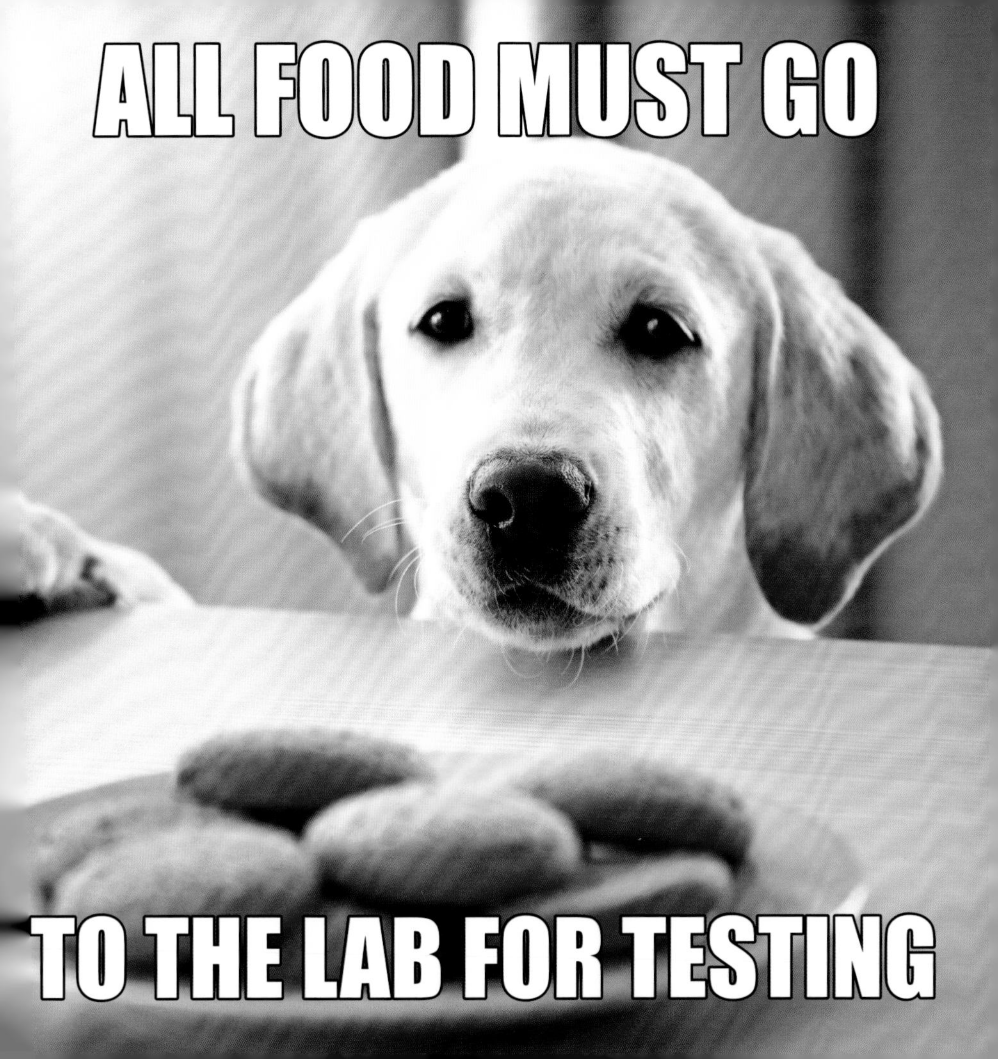
ALL FOOD MUST GO
TO THE LAB FOR TESTING

THIS SCALE MUST BE IN
OUNCES, RIGHT?

COME ON INNER PEACE
I DON'T HAVE ALL DAY

DON'T BE PEANUT BUTTER AND JEALOUS.

AND YOU SAID WE WERE

GOING TO THE PARK

THIS IS A SPA DAY SO...

MOVE ALONG, PLEASE

NOT SURE IF IT'S

LAZY SATURDAY OR LAZY SUNDAY

DAMN. I'M SEXY AS HELL

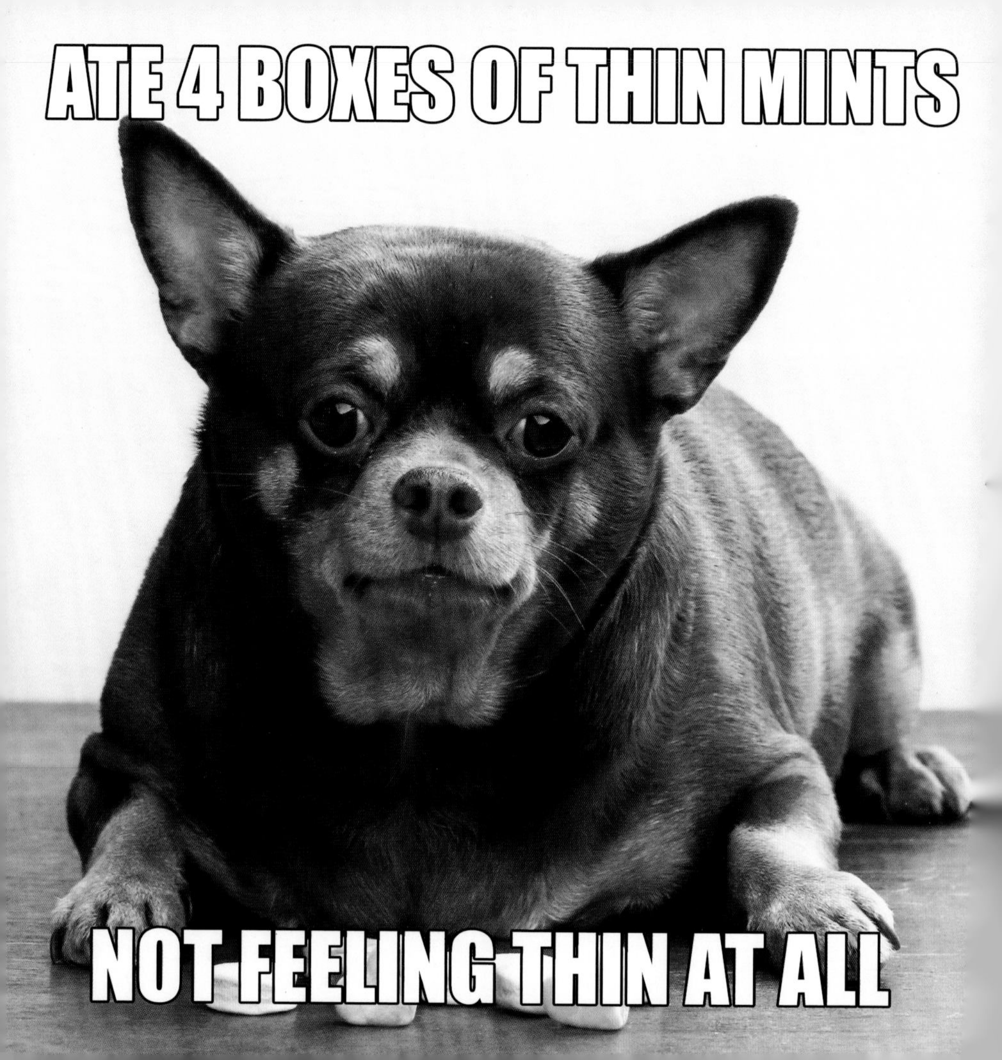
ATE 4 BOXES OF THIN MINTS
NOT FEELING THIN AT ALL

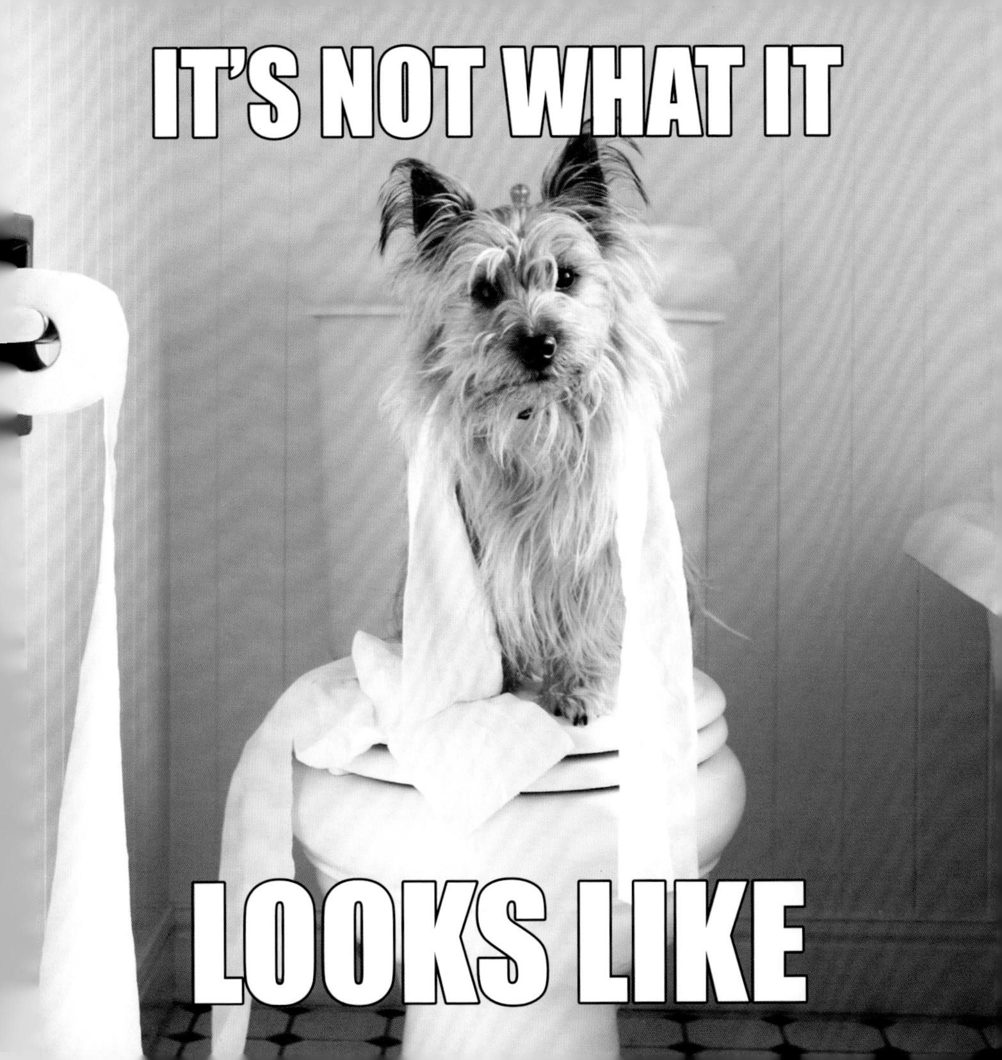
IT'S NOT WHAT IT
LOOKS LIKE

WHEN YOU WAKE UP AND REALIZE IT'S NOT THE WEEKEND

LIKE YOU THOUGHT IT WAS

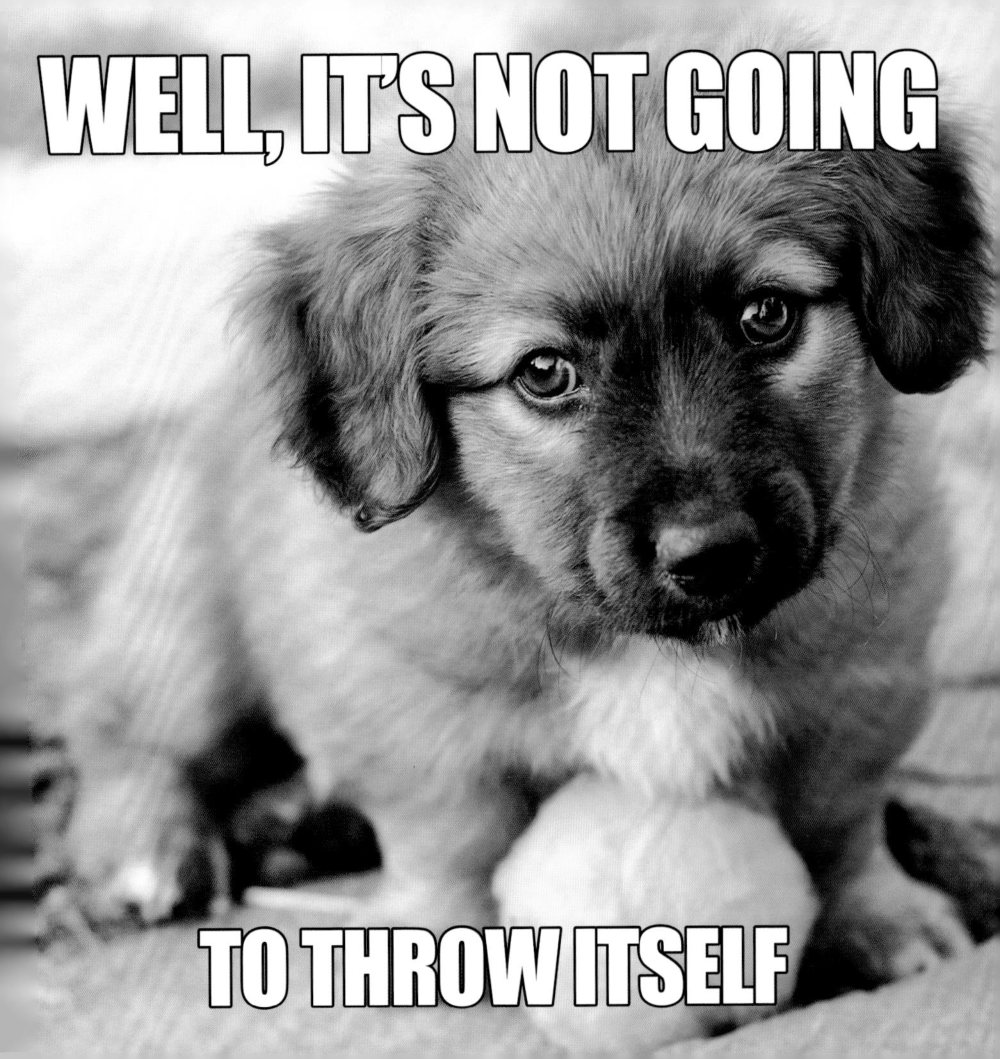
WELL, IT'S NOT GOING
TO THROW ITSELF

IT'S CALLED FASHION

EVER HEARD OF IT?

I MISSED MY 5:00 NAP

NOW I HAVE TO WAIT
FOR MY 5:15 NAP

WOW, YOU RAN A MARATHON?

HOW HEAVY WAS THE SLED?

LEAVE NO CRUMB BEHIND

BLOCKING OUT
THE HATERS

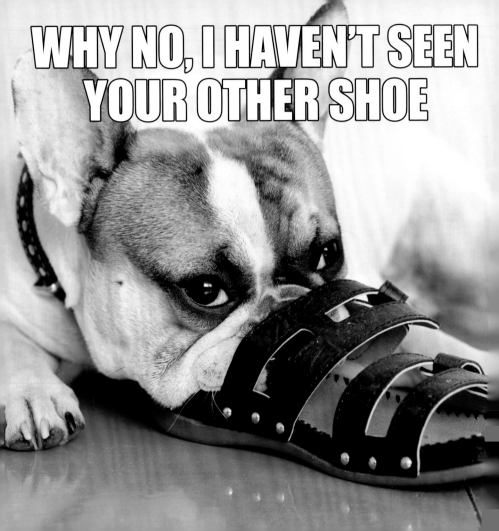

DO WANT!!

COFFEE CANNOT FIX

THIS KIND OF TIRED

SELF CONTROL
LEVEL: EXPERT

I SEE YOU DIDN'T DELETE

YOUR BROWSER HISTORY